Original title:
Wandering in the Wildwood

Copyright © 2025 Creative Arts Management OÜ
All rights reserved.

Author: Tobias Winslow
ISBN HARDBACK: 978-1-80567-380-4
ISBN PAPERBACK: 978-1-80567-679-9

Rapture in the Rustling Grasses

Bumblebees buzzing, what a sight,
Dancing through flowers, oh what delight.
A squirrel stumbles, trips on a root,
Laughing at nature in this silly suit.

Sunlight dapples, tickles my face,
Bunnies hop by, join the chase.
Frogs wear tuxedos, croak at the moon,
Singing their tunes, a funny cartoon.

Nature's Palette Unveiled

A canvas of colors, bright and bizarre,
Fruits hang like ornaments, a nature bazaar.
Pinecones tumble like mischievous sprites,
Painting the ground with their quirky bites.

The wind tells jokes with a playful breeze,
Whispering secrets to giggling trees.
A ladybug prances, steadfast and spry,
In this funny realm, where birds wear ties.

Chasing Echoes Beyond the Trail

Footsteps crunch on a path so spry,
Echoes laugh back, oh me, oh my!
A deer photobombs, strikes a pose,
Nature's own star with antlers that glow.

Snakes in sunbathing, doing the twist,
Frolicking flowers, can't resist.
A tree stump winks, a jester so grand,
In this hilarious forest, nothing's quite planned.

Rooted in the Moment

Mushrooms giggle, doing the dance,
While chipmunks prattle—what a chance!
Grasshoppers leap with a twist and a flip,
Nature's circus, never a trip.

Captured by wonder, the sky painted blue,
Clouds are sheep that prance on cue.
A sigh from the earth, with laughter it hums,
Living in joy, as the wilderness drums.

Quiet Revelations in the Glade

Amidst the trees, I lost my way,
Chasing squirrels who'd rather play.
They giggled loud, I tripped on roots,
While wearing mismatched hiking boots.

The ferns were tall, they whispered there,
"Get off the trail, you silly bear!"
A bird remarked, with quite the flair,
"You're more lost than a rubber hair!"

The Spirit of Ancient Grove

The old oak tree danced with the breeze,
I asked it kindly, "Got any keys?"
"To unlock fun, or tree-shaped treats?"
It creaked with laughter, "Try the sweets!"

A gnarled root pretended to snore,
"Don't wake me up, I found a bore!"
But when I slipped on acorns round,
The whole grove burst with joyous sound!

Paths of Enchantment and Mystery

The path before me was thick with charm,
A fairy waved, "You mean no harm?"
"Keep your snacks close, the ants will dance,"
A squirrel winked, "You'll lose your pants!"

The whispers teased through leaves above,
While mossy stones winked with much love.
I followed trails of lost green socks,
Where giggling shadows set their clocks!

Fragments of a Nature Lover's Dream

In fields of flowers, I skipped with glee,
A bee buzzed by, said, "Join my spree!"
  "It's bumbly fun, but do take care,"
  "Avoid the hats, they're full of hair!"

The sun played peek-a-boo with clouds,
As chipmunks gathered in silly crowds.
  I tried to frolic in floral streams,
But tripped on roots, ruining my dreams!

Fragile Moments in the Understory

A squirrel stole my sandwich, what a cheek!
I chased it through the brambles, a bit of a freak.
It giggled as it jumped, quite the bold little brat,
I guess it thought my lunch was more fun than that.

The trees above were grumbling, judging my plight,
While the birds chuckled softly, oh what a sight.
I swore I'd get my feast back, a mission so grand,
But alas, I found a mushroom and sat down to stand.

The Book of Trees and Time

In pages made of bark, the stories are steep,
Of owls who gossip while the world is asleep.
A pine tried to recite, lost its voice in the breeze,
And laughed at its mishap, shaking slow wooden knees.

The oak told me secrets, which were quite dull,
He rattled on loudly, too proud to be full.
I giggled at his tales of roots and of shade,
And offered him a blanket, but he just swayed.

Emulations of the Untamed Heart

The wildflowers danced as I tripped on a rock,
They whispered 'look out!' but I just couldn't stop.
A bee buzzed my ear, gave me quite the scare,
I ducked and I dodged like a clumsy old hare.

Around me, the ferns giggled, so green and so sly,
As I flailed like a dancer beneath the blue sky.
I vowed to be graceful, to leap light and free,
But elbows collided with the nearest tall tree.

Dreams among the Shadows

In twilight's soft glow, the shadows grew long,
They whispered of mischief, and sang silly songs.
A raccoon in a top hat thought he ruled the night,
He bowled with fallen acorns, what a curious sight!

I laughed as he stumbled, tripped over his tail,
The fireflies flickered, sparkles in the pale.
A party of critters took over the glen,
While I tried to be quiet, again and again.

The Enchanted Trail Awaits

Beneath the leafy boughs we prance,
With squirrels playing peek-a-boo by chance.
We trip on roots, oh what a sight!
The forest giggles, day turns to night.

A map that leads to nowhere found,
With fairies laughing all around.
A compass spins, it's upside down,
We end up lost without a frown.

Lost in the Green Immensity

In a jungle gym of twisted vines,
We lose our way, oh how it shines!
A raccoon holds a party here,
With snacks and riddles, never fear!

We follow a trail of flowered socks,
While teasing birds that wear their smocks.
Each turn reveals a silly sight,
A frog in a crown, oh what a delight!

Dappled Sunlight and Shadows

In beams of gold, we dance and skip,
With tree branches ready for a sip.
We catch a glimpse of a dancing hare,
Who shows us moves with great flair!

The shadows play hide and seek,
While a woodpecker gives a cheeky peek.
Mushrooms giggle underfoot,
As we twirl in our wild pursuit!

The Call of the Verdant Unknown

Through bramble and thicket, we make our way,
Disguised in laughter, come what may.
A wise old owl with glasses, you see,
Offers advice on how to be silly!

With leaves as hats and sticks as wands,
We declare ourselves the forest's fronds.
As butterflies join in our playful cheer,
We dance till the stars appear!

Revelations Beneath the Stars

In the night, raccoons debate,
Should paths be straight or just tempting fate?
While owls hoot wisdom in rhymes,
The fireflies dance, provoking their chimes.

A squirrel claims to be quite a king,
While tightening his acorn bling.
Chasing shadows, they trip and collide,
Where laughter and mischief collide side by side.

Beneath the glow of a crescent moon,
A frog croons, thinks he's a tune.
The trees giggle, an ancient glee,
As nature's jesters put on a spree.

In a field, a butterfly flirts,
While a deer in the headlights just squirts!
With nature's chorus in hearty cheer,
The wildwood is hilariously clear.

In the Heart of Nature's Repose

Where lazy bees buzz in the sun,
A turtle races, thinking it's fun.
The foxes play tag, sharp and spry,
While the grasses sway with a gentle sigh.

A bear dreams of honey's great debate,
While the raccoons show up way too late.
With fruits in hand, their stash is grand,
Yet one drops a berry and's banned from the band!

Clouds drift by, waiting for a jest,
As chipmunks plot to put patience to test.
Politely, the owls offer their cheers,
For a night filled with stumbles and silly jeers.

Beneath an oak where laughter descends,
Frogs croak the melody, their choppy blends.
Nature winks at the stories that bloom,
In her heart, chaos makes room!

The Lure of the Hidden Grove

In a thicket of laughter close to the stream,
A rabbit proposes the ultimate scheme.
To tickle the fox with a feathered joke,
Hilarity follows, all branches evoke.

A squirrel takes charge, with great zeal,
While a wise old toad tries to conceal.
The path of mischief evolving every hour,
Becomes a delightful, ungoverned power.

Vines become swings in this wild ride,
Numerous giggles are swept in the tide.
As shadows bounce and the daylight wanes,
Laughter resonates, it's joy that remains.

In the grove, nothing's ever what it seems,
A dance of the fireflies endless dreams.
Chasing light, we tumble and play,
Where sunlight cradles laughter each day.

Quest for the Sylvan Spirit

On a path where mischief weaves and sways,
A hedgehog recounts his scrambled days.
With laughter echoing through the glen,
Creatures unite and assemble again.

A wandering minstrel sings of a feast,
As woodpeckers drum their raucous beast.
The whispers of pine twist hilariously,
Dropping secrets and giggles so seriously.

At dusk, when shadows start to prance,
A bigfoot attempts the moonlight dance.
In wild jubilation, all nature joins,
With humor as fuel, they paint the coins.

Sending spirits into a tizzy so bright,
They all gather 'round to celebrate night.
In pockets of laughter, nature glees,
The quest is just fun, as lightness frees!

Encounters in the Realm of Green

In the shade of trees so tall,
Squirrels chatter, heed my call.
A bear slipped by, a little shy,
I waved hello, and so did I.

A rabbit danced with clumsy feet,
While toads hummed tunes, oh what a treat!
A raccoon, with a curious stare,
Stole my snack without a care.

The owls hooted, quite bemused,
As I stumbled, feeling quite abused.
A deer tiptoed, shaking its head,
As I tripped over roots and fled.

In green realms full of jest and glee,
Nature plays tricks, oh can't you see?
So I'll laugh with friends, big and small,
In this wild world, we'll share it all.

The Breath of Earth and Sky

The breeze whispers secrets so grand,
While ants march, forming their band.
A butterfly, so bold and bright,
Flew through my nose, oh what a fright!

The clouds laughed down, fluffy and white,
As I stumbled in awkward flight.
A fox snickered, tucked in a tree,
Challenging my clumsiness with glee.

Raindrops tickled, playful as can be,
While mushrooms giggled, just wait and see!
The sun peeked out, a cheeky grin,
As I splashed in puddles, yielding to sin.

With every hiccup in this dance,
The wildwood offers a funny chance.
To trip, to slip, and oh to glide,
In nature's arms, I'll laugh with pride.

Lost Among the Whispering Boughs

I took a turn way too brisk,
Now trees laugh loud, what a risk!
A squirrel mocks, doing a spin,
As I ask, 'Where do I begin?'

Branches wave, it's quite the show,
Critters trading in gossip flow.
A chipmunk bursts into a song,
I can't help but hum along.

Lost in twists, a maze of green,
Where pinecones tumble, what a scene!
A bushy-tailed friend giggles near,
As I contemplate my sense of steer.

In shadows deep, hilarity reigns,
Nature's humor, in her veins.
I'll dance with joy, suspending woe,
In this realm of laughs, I'll surely grow.

Secrets Beneath the Canopy

Under a dome of leafy dreams,
The world unfolds with silly themes.
A raccoon plots with mischievous flair,
While I corner myself in thin air.

Mushrooms wiggle, peeking out,
While frogs croak secrets, oh what about?
Trees lean in, sharing their tales,
Of clumsy friends on fluffy trails.

A parrot chats, never shy,
Making jokes that make me cry.
As I tumble, a root afoot,
The laughter echoes, sharp and soot.

So here I am, beneath the green,
Where silly moments reign supreme.
I'll laugh with fauna, wild and free,
Dancing in shadows, just wait and see!

Tangles of Time and Terrain

Lost my shoe in a muddy pit,
Chased by squirrels, they just won't quit.
Tripped on a branch, fell with a thud,
Got a face full of leafy sludge.

Tangled vines, oh what a sight,
A dance with shadows in the night.
Wicked roots with a sense of glee,
Laughing at me—was it just a tree?

A Pilgrim's Heart in the Thickets

Stumbled across a bouncy hare,
He winked at me, like he just didn't care.
Raccoons in hats playing games of chance,
Who knew the woods had such wild romance?

A feathered choir sings way up high,
Mocking my efforts, oh me, oh my!
With every step, the ground shifts and rolls,
But laughter bubbles where the wild heart strolls.

Whispers Among the Tall Pines

Tall pines gossip in the gentle breeze,
Telling tales of mischief, if you please.
I heard a critter try to catch a snack,
Only to drop it—what a comical hack!

The squirrels hold court with acorn crowns,
While branches bob like they're town-bound clowns.
Nature's jesters play tricks by design,
In this forest realm, it's hard to feel fine.

In the Embrace of Earth's Beauty

Sunshine rains down like glittering cheer,
Flowers giggle, I swear I can hear.
A turtle in shades moves oh-so-slow,
While a froggy friend steals the star of the show.

Grinning rocks sit, proud on their perch,
While worms throw a party—what a weird search!
I joined in the fun with a clumsy twist,
In this wild parade, how could I resist?

Finding Home in the Wilderness

A squirrel stole my sandwich,
And laughed with glee, oh dear!
I chased him up a tree,
He waved, 'Thanks for the beer!'

Branches nudged my forehead,
As I tripped over a root.
A raccoon gave me side-eye,
And said, 'You're quite the hoot!'

An owl tried to guide me,
With wisdom far and wide.
But I found an acorn,
That got stuck in my stride.

I twirled with a fern,
While beetles danced nearby.
In this green circus, folks,
I'm the star of the sky!

The Path Less Taken Call

I discovered a path,
That led me to a stream.
With frogs in tuxedos,
They twirled in a grand dream.

A butterfly sneezed,
And caused a major fuss,
I slipped on some moss,
While befriending a bush!

Lost in this green maze,
With critters holding court,
They declared me their king,
As I danced in a sort.

The trees clapped their leaves,
To the beat of my fall.
Each twist I take, I laugh,
At the wild's joyful call!

Haikus of the Hidden Eden

Fungi in top hats,
Waltzing under silver beams,
Nature's grand soirée.

Whispers of the breeze,
Critters gossiping in style,
Squirrels play charades.

Mushrooms hold the jokes,
As ferns fan them with delight,
The pine trees all laugh.

While I trip and fall,
They giggle, strike a pose, too,
Nature's comedy.

Flickering Shadows Upon the Resting Earth

Shadows dance in glee,
As the sun bids day farewell.
A raccoon's a star,
In this nighttime cabaret.

Fireflies play tricks,
While mocking my silly hat,
I wave back with pride,
'You're bright, but how 'bout that?'

Crickets hold the mics,
For their nightly serenade,
While grass stands up tall,
To cheer at every note played.

Flickering and bright,
The wildwood's humor shines,
In laughter and light,
The night stays in good vines.

Revelations in the Green Abyss

I stumbled upon a squirrel in a hat,
It cackled and scolded, 'You're too fat!'
He offered me acorns, a fine gourmet,
I waved him off with a loud 'no way!'

The frogs held a concert but sang off tune,
I clapped for their courage, like a buffoon.
The trees whispered secrets, 'Don't carry a snack,'
Lest a raccoon shows up and starts the attack!

Verses of the Nature's Chorus

The bees wore tiny coats, looking quite neat,
Dancing in circles, oh what a feat!
An owl popped up, claiming to be wise,
But got startled by shadows, to my surprise!

The butterflies gossiped of flowers and sun,
While I tripped over roots, thinking this fun.
A skunk gave a wink, said, 'Don't take a whiff,'
With laughter I left him, that scent was no gift!

Boundless Browsing Beneath the Sky

I found a lost shoe, engraved 'To my mate!',
Next to a bear who seemed quite sedate.
He grinned as I shuffled, my foot found its place,
But alas, it was soggy and smelled of disgrace!

A parrot demanded I tell him a joke,
He squawked with delight, then a branch he broke.
I laughed as he flapped, a true comedic sight,
Turning the forest into open mic night!

A Stroll Through the Enchanted Realm

The path was all twisty, a real maze of trees,
Where gnomes peeked out, drinking herbal teas.
They offered me biscuits, just one or a few,
But I feared they'd trap me, so politely I flew!

I found a chipmunk, a real chatty chap,
Said his favorite hobby was taking long naps.
With laughter we shared, under skies full of charm,
In this wild place, there's never a qualm!

Treading Softly on Nature's Canvas

I tiptoe through the forest shade,
Where trees have secrets, softly laid.
I'll step on snails and chatter with bees,
They giggle as I dance with ease.

The flowers blush when I pass by,
I swear they wink, I'll never lie.
A squirrel mocks with a cheeky grin,
As I trip over roots, where do I begin?

The brook asks, 'Do you see the frogs?'
I nod and laugh at their silly jigs.
I'm painting footprints in this art,
Nature's gallery, a quirky part.

Oh, what a show, oh what a play!
With every turn, I find a way
To dance and twirl on soft green grass,
The wildwood stage, a merry mass.

The Melodies of Hidden Hollows

In tiny nooks where shadows dwell,
I heard a bird, oh what a swell!
It crooned to me a silly tune,
I laughed so hard, I burst a balloon!

The owls are hooting in surprise,
They roll their eyes and shake their thighs.
A rabbit hops, thinks it's a show,
'Disco's back!' it seems to crow.

Each leaf has stories, all in sync,
Nature's choir, what do you think?
A caterpillar joins the song,
With a wiggle, it won't be long!

As day turns into twilight's glow,
The critters jam, putting on a show.
I sway along with all my friends,
In these hollow spaces, laughter never ends.

Skipping Stones in Solitude

By the bank, I found a stone,
'Come here,' it said, 'you're not alone!'
I tossed it forth with hopeful might,
But it sank deep without a fight.

A turtle laughed as it strolled by,
'You call that skipping? Oh, my, oh my!'
I grinned and tried to throw again,
The splash was grand, like thunder's din.

The frogs croaked back, with roars so loud,
They formed a ruckus, oh, so proud!
A majestic leap from way up high,
And down it splashed, with a funny sigh.

So here I play, no need for fame,
Just stones and giggles in this game.
With every hit, the laughter grows,
In this leafy realm where time flows slow.

The Embrace of Nature's Veil

The breeze today is feeling cheeky,
It tugs at leaves, oh so sneaky!
I swear it whispers, 'Dance with glee,'
As branches sway around me free.

A bear in berries can't help but smirk,
I join the fun, it's quite the perk!
In shades of green, we play peek-a-boo,
'Come join us, friend,' the wildwood crew!

The faeries giggle as they dart,
'This wild embrace is quite the art!'
With every step, I trip and shout,
Nature's humor is what it's about.

So here we laugh in this vast domain,
With every tickle of the rain.
Under nature's veil, so divine,
I find my place, where jokes intertwine.

A Symphony of Rustling Leaves

In the trees, a chatter grows,
Squirrels gossip, striking poses.
Branches dance, a merry tune,
As acorns tumble from their noon.

Frogs sing out a croaky song,
While bees buzz by and flaunt their throng.
A raccoon winks with mischief bright,
As shadows play, embracing night.

Breezes tease the skittish fawn,
Leaves rustle softly, dusk till dawn.
A picnic spread? Oh, what a jest!
Ants have feasted; we're the guests!

With giggles and sighs of delight,
Even owls hoot at this sight.
In nature's dance, we can't resist,
Join the fun; we can't be missed!

Beneath the Starlit Canopy

Underneath the twinkling show,
Fireflies flash like disco glow.
Hiccups rise from a nearby creek,
What's that noise? A chipmunk's squeak!

Napping bears snore in delight,
While raccoons plot a snack tonight.
Stars point out the best dessert,
A berry pie? Oh, what a flirt!

Crickets join the nighttime band,
Each note a bump, each beat a stand.
A bear in pajamas? Quite absurd,
Moonlit laughter, rarely heard.

In this playground, wild and bright,
Every shadow dances with light.
Under stars, we spin and sway,
In moonlight's laughter, we'll forever stay!

Thorns and Thickets of Discovery

Oh, thorny path, a prickly plight,
Finding treasures feels so right!
Each branch that swats my face like this,
Leaves me yearning for a blissful kiss.

Hedgehogs snooze amidst the bramble,
While bees, oh my, they love to scramble.
We dodge the thorns, oh what a game,
Nature's puzzles, never the same.

A rusted can becomes a prize,
Old boots whisper with surprise.
In tangled joys, we laugh so free,
Merry patches, looks just like me!

With slapstick moments, joy does bloom,
While shadows chase us round the room.
In the thicket, laughter roars,
As every journey opens doors!

The Enchantment of Mossy Trails

On trails adorned with velvet green,
Mossy carpets, a comical scene.
Wobbly steps and giggles fly,
Do mushrooms dance? Oh, my oh my!

A sneaky snail slides by with glee,
As I trip over roots like a bee.
Dunked in laughter at each small fall,
Nature's comedy, welcome to all!

The sun peeks through the leafy veil,
While squirrels giggle, plotting a tale.
A squirrel drop? Oh what a blast—
Let's aim for laughter, we'll have a blast!

With every turn, a playful twist,
In the woods, we can't resist.
This enchanted path, wild and free,
In its embrace, just you and me!

The Call of the Unseen

In the forest, shadows prance,
Squirrels plotting their next dance.
Mushrooms giggle, ants parade,
While the tree trunks trade charades.

A fox with glasses reads a tome,
"Is this my path? Or safe to roam?"
A parrot drops a feathery quip,
As the deer joins in for a trip.

Beneath the branches, laughter grows,
As raccoons wear their finest clothes.
The owls wink and hoot with glee,
Secret jokes just for the trees.

So, take a step in leafy haze,
Where laughing leaves twist in a daze.
The unseen calls, a laugh it brings,
In this realm where nonsense sings.

Serenity in the Shaded Glens

In the glens where shadows play,
Bunnies grind their paws all day.
Chirping birds in suits galore,
Debating which tree holds the score.

A turtle lost, takes quite the pause,
In his shell, he finds applause.
"I'm no racer!" he proclaims loud,
As the rabbits leap and form a crowd.

Then comes the breeze, a playful tease,
Tickling leaves, dancing with ease.
The sun winks down, quite pleased to see,
A ticklish dance — oh, come and flee!

With every rustle, chuckles flare,
In shaded glens, a jovial air.
Nature's whimsy, pure delight,
Life's a joke, so laugh all night!

Where the Wildflowers Sing

In fields where petals laugh and sway,
Bees debate on how to play.
A poppy prances, a daisy spins,
Nature's dance, where joy begins.

Hedgehogs roll in pansies bright,
Spreading cheer in colors light.
While butterflies tell jokes in flight,
Tip their wings to the morning light.

Frogs croak tunes, a serenade,
As lily pads form a grand parade.
Funny frogs in top hats croon,
Their laughter rising to the moon.

So come and join this flowery scene,
Where every bloom wears a crown of green.
In laughter's arms, we shall reside,
In this garden where giggles glide.

Chasing Sunbeams Through the Thicket

Through thickets thick, the sunlight beams,
A raccoon plots his daylight schemes.
With a wink and a hat askew,
He raises a toast to the morning dew.

The hedgehogs race in silly lines,
With mismatched socks, and silly signs.
"Catch me!" cries one, as he bounces back,
Into a bush, without a snack.

The ferns giggle underfoot,
As a lost shoe forms a merry root.
A fox in sneakers, and a grin so wide,
Chasing shadows on a sunny ride.

So run and play, join the fun,
In every ray, life has begun.
Through thickets deep, we'll laugh and spin,
In the wild, where joy is kin.

Reflections in the Forest Pool

In a pond so bubbling bright,
I saw my face, quite a sight!
A frog hopped on, gave me a grin,
Said, 'You look better with frog skin!'

The leaves above had quite the show,
Dancing like they knew how to flow.
I tried to join; oh, what a sight!
Tripped on a root—what a delight!

A fish laughed as it swam on by,
I told it jokes; oh me, oh my!
The trees just chuckled, lost in their thoughts,
Nature's humor, tied in knots!

I splashed the water, caused a big splash,
Reflections wobbled in a wild dash.
The forest giggled, oh, such a tease,
In the pool where mirth does not cease!

A Tapestry of Nature's Wonders

The flowers wear their colors bright,
They sway and dance, what a sight!
Bumblebees buzz with a clumsy cheer,
They've had too much nectar, it's clear!

The trees all chat, their bark a bit coarse,
Sharing tales of the wild, their main discourse.
A squirrel dashed by with snacks galore,
Dropping acorns—what a chore!

The sun popped out, then played shy,
Behind the clouds, oh, what a guy!
A raccoon winked, reminding me,
"Snack time's better when you're free!"

In this gallery where laughter grows,
Nature stitches smiles in a row.
I'll be the thread, tangled but bold,
In this tapestry that never gets old!

Crossroads of the Heart and Earth

At the crossroads, I stood and spun,
Two paths ahead, which one's more fun?
One led to a mushroom party, hooray!
The other—oh no! Just fading away!

A hedgehog said, 'Choose wisely, friend,'
With a laugh that seemed to never end.
I picked the path with glowworms' light,
A party with snacks? Oh, what a delight!

The fungi danced in their colorful shoes,
Teaching me their fun little moves.
With every twirl, I lost my mind,
In this wild magic, joy I find!

Yet lurking behind a bush so near,
A shy little fox whispered, 'Stay clear!'
But I led the dance, with a dash and a jig,
In this heart of the wood, I grow ever big!

The Hidden Language of the Woods

The trees talk softly in whispers and sighs,
Sharing secrets under the brightening skies.
A wily old owl hoots out a pun,
While a rabbit rolls over—oh, what fun!

Mushrooms giggle, sprouting with grace,
As the wind rushes through, a playful embrace.
A lizard fetches a wish from a breeze,
Promising fortunes to those who tease!

The brook babbles jokes, its current so spry,
Jesting with frogs who leap high and dry.
The flowers reply with a giggle so sweet,
In this hidden language, life's melody beats!

As I sit and listen, the forest completes,
A chorus of laughter, a symphony of treats.
In this green theater, they play on still,
Oh, the joys of nature, always a thrill!

Journey Through the Whispering Pines

In the forest where the squirrels play,
I lost my hat, it ran away!
The trees chuckled, the branches swung,
A feather stuck, oh what a tongue!

Beneath the boughs, the shadows creep,
I tripped on roots, and fell in heap.
A raccoon looked, gave me a grin,
Said, "Looks like fun, now let's begin!"

The owls hooted with a cheeky glee,
They must have known they'd laugh at me.
A log rolled by, oh how it danced,
I couldn't help but join its prance!

As I zoomed past the bushes green,
I met a fox who slyly preened.
"Care for a laugh?" he slyly winked,
"Just watch your step, or you'll be linked!"

Beneath the Boughs of Mystery

Beneath the branches, shadows play,
I saw a gnome, he looked my way.
His hat was big, his beard was wide,
He chuckled low, then tried to hide!

A path appeared, all twisty turns,
Where mushrooms danced and sunlight burns.
I took a leap, a twig did crack,
A chipmunk laughed, then ran right back!

The breeze played tunes with whistling leaves,
While squirrels plotted in their thieves.
I joined the chatter, their jokes took flight,
Near a fat toadstool, oh what a sight!

Fairies peeked, with mischief bright,
They whispered, "Chase that moonlit light!"
But all I caught was a bramble's sting,
Still, I laughed, what joy they'd bring!

Solitude Among the Ferns

Among soft ferns, I laid my head,
Thought I was lost, but then I said,
"If I'm alone, then make it grand,"
A curious snail took up my hand.

With crickets chirping, I broke a trance,
Joined in their song, a little dance.
They looked amazed, all green and bright,
"Who knew a human could take flight?"

Then through the leaves, a shadow leapt,
A friendly deer who slyly crept.
She sniffed my shoe, then made a dash,
Can't say I didn't enjoy the clash!

The ferns stood still, in giggles rife,
Where every leaf brought playful life.
I soared with joy, did not give in,
In solitude, the fun begins!

Footfalls on Forgotten Soil

In ancient woods, where whispers call,
I tripped on roots and made a sprawl.
The leaves guffawed, the branches bent,
"Oh, look at him!" they all lament!

With each footfall, a critter fled,
A parade of bugs danced overhead.
I waved at them, they waved me back,
A wobbly shuffle, what a whack!

The mossy ground, a fluffy bed,
Oh, how I giggled, "Shall we spread?"
Then blooms peeked out and swayed in cheer,
My wild mishaps brought them near!

An ant parade formed a small line,
I joined the ranks, felt so divine.
The sun then set, the moon turned bright,
In this odd crew, I'd find delight!

A Symphony of Rustling Leaves

In trees that giggle and sway,
A squirrel drops acorns today.
The birds are busy in their glee,
Chasing shadows, wild and free.

Mushrooms whisper silly tales,
While breezes play in leafy veils.
A raccoon juggles shiny scraps,
As laughter bursts from hidden traps.

Crickets serenade the night,
With a rhythm quite a sight.
Owls hoot jokes that twist and spin,
Laughing at the moon's cheeky grin.

So join the frolic, join the fun,
In this green world where we all run.
With every giggle, every cheer,
The wildwood's humor draws us near.

Pathways Among the Ancient Giants

Beneath the boughs of towering trees,
Where roots tangle like old fairies.
A deer wears glasses, quite a sight,
Reading recipes by candlelight.

The paths weave tales both old and strange,
Where shadows play, and notions change.
A chipmunk dons a tiny hat,
Debating why the sky is flat.

Around the bend by mossy stones,
The toads are hosting late night phones.
They're breaking news of bugs that dance,
Inviting all for one last chance.

With every step, the stories grow,
In this land where laughs overflow.
Each giant's whisper, a hidden jest,
In this realm where humor's the best.

Dreams of the Woodland Realm

In a land where the laughter grows,
Mice are painting on their toes.
The stars are chips of happy cheese,
Falling gently with the breeze.

Squirrel spies a climbing vine,
Thinking it might just be divine.
He climbs and slips with quite a flair,
Tumbling down without a care.

Foxes tell tales of myths and dreams,
While fireflies light up their schemes.
A badger's doing cartwheels bold,
As tales of wildwood laughter unfold.

Underneath the silver moon,
Crickets play a merry tune.
With each note, the woods alight,
In this realm of pure delight.

The Dance of the Twilit Glade

In the glade where shadows prance,
Tiny creatures join the dance.
A hedgehog spins with striped attire,
His feet a blur, he's quick as fire.

Frogs leap high in joyful leaps,
Chasing dreams that make them squeak.
While butterflies with giggles race,
Painting smiles all over the place.

The flowers sway with cheerful poise,
Swaying sweetly to the noise.
A bear plays drums on hollow logs,
Echoing laughs through lamplight fogs.

As twilight blankets all in fun,
The woodland party's just begun.
Every step, a joyful cheer,
In this glade, there's nothing to fear.

Echoes of Untamed Paths

A squirrel scurries up the tree,
Chasing dreams of nuts and glee.
With every leap, it seems to shout,
'Just one more snack, then I'll come out!'

A rabbit hops, its ears a-flap,
While raccoons plan a midnight cap.
They giggle as they steal some gems,
From picnic sites of hapless friends.

The babbling brook hums a tune,
As frogs croak out their afternoon.
Each melody, a joyful jibe,
Nature's jesters, full of vibe.

When night descends, the owls begin,
Trading tales of ancient sin.
'What's that? A fox in a tuxedo?'
'No! Just my friend, the witty weirdo!'

Shadows Dance in Green Embrace

Underneath the leafy veil,
A chipmunk weaves a comical tale.
With tiny paws, it grabs a treat,
A stash of acorns, oh so sweet!

The shadows twirl in playful glee,
While butterflies sip on nectar tea.
A bumblebee buzzes by, so bold,
Dressed in stripes of black and gold.

A thistle tickles a passing hare,
As laughter ripples through the air.
The breeze plays tricks, it twirls and spins,
Nature giggles while the day begins.

Fragrant flowers sway and clap,
As starlings hold a feathered rap.
Each step beneath the emerald dome,
Reveals that wild is truly home.

The Lure of Solitary Trails

On a path of twists and turns,
A bouncy toad with laughter yearns.
With every hop, it plays a song,
Igniting joy all day long.

The trees high-five the passing breeze,
While critters play tag with utmost ease.
A snail slides by with regal flair,
Pondering life without a care.

Each bend reveals a silly sight,
A deer in shades, donning delight.
It winks and prances on its way,
Sharing giggles throughout the day.

Field mice host a dance parade,
Set to rhythms that they've made.
With flowers as their disco lights,
Nature's fun spills into nights.

Nature's Silent Invitation

In the woods, a funny scene,
A hedgehog juggles, if you've seen!
With tiny balls of moss and glee,
He's the champion of the spree.

As trees stand tall, they whisper low,
To sleepy bears, just take it slow.
A raccoon waves a furry hand,
Inviting all to join the band.

The midnight moon, a spotlight bright,
Frogs leap high in pure delight.
They croak their tunes, a funky beat,
Dancing paws and wiggly feet!

So, join the fun beneath the stars,
Where laughter echoes, near and far.
In this wild, enchanted land,
Nature's jesters take their stand.

Spirits of the Wandering Trail

In the woods, I met a hare,
Wearing boots and showing flair.
He hopped and danced, a splendid sight,
Claiming he could beat me in a fight.

A squirrel challenged him to race,
With acorns flying all over the place.
They tripped and stumbled, round and round,
As laughter echoed through the ground.

A raccoon joined with a bag of snacks,
Claiming that he'd bring us back.
But when he stretched to grab a peach,
He flipped and fell – oh what a speech!

The forest giggled with glee so bright,
As creatures gathered for a night.
With haunted tales of silly fright,
We spun our stories by the light.

Tales Told by Twisting Vines

The ivy whispered secrets low,
Of a snail who wore a disco bow.
He spun and twirled with such delight,
While frogs croaked tunes to steal the night.

A parrot perched above the scene,
Sang of missed worms, oh so keen.
His voice wasn't smooth, but full of fun,
As he tried to dance like he was the one.

The vines, like sprites, curled and swayed,
Crafting stories that never betrayed.
A butterfly with polka dots bright,
Flashed tales of dancing till moonlight.

In this tangled wood where jesters roam,
Each twist and turn felt like home.
With laughter bubbling, life's carefree,
The stories of vines, forever free.

Guiding Light in the Forest

A firefly flicked its tiny glow,
Leading me where I wouldn't go.
With giggles and shouts, like tiny bells,
I followed it through hidden spells.

The moon peered down with a smirk,
As I stumbled over an old piece of work.
A gopher popped out to say, "Hey there!"
"Try not to trip, you're going nowhere!"

A wise old owl, perched up high,
Said, "Life's too short to just pass by."
He was reading a book upside down,
Wearing a very silly frown.

With each misstep, laughter soared,
In this wood where joy was stored.
We danced under trees, wild and free,
Chasing shadows, just you and me.

A Journey Through Verdant Echoes

In a clearing where daisies played,
A tap-dancing beetle unafraid.
He shimmied and shook, the leaf's delight,
While crickets joined in for the night.

A wise old tree, with bark so grand,
Said, "Join the show, and take my hand."
I laughed as it jiggled, roots in a twist,
With every shake, I couldn't resist.

A family of hedgehogs rolled near,
Playing ball with glee and cheer.
I almost joined in with a tumble,
But instead, I fell – down I fumble!

The echoes of laughter filled the air,
As woodland creatures danced without a care.
In this green world where giggles reign,
We'll roam forever, again and again.

The Wild Song of the Brook

A brook sings loud, a playful shout,
Rocks are its drums, no doubt about.
Frogs leap high, in silly dance,
Splashing water, taking a chance.

Fish poke heads, just for a peek,
Whispers of secrets, soft and sleek.
Each swirl and bubble, a jolly tune,
Nature's party starts at noon.

Leaves shake with laughter, branches sway,
Squirrels giggle, come out to play.
A turtle grins, then takes a nap,
While insects buzz, a tiny clap.

So come along, let your heart soar,
Dance with the brook, and you'll want more!
Jump and skip, don't be too shy,
Embrace the fun beneath the sky.

A Haven Beneath Foliage

Beneath the trees, the world feels bright,
Sitting on roots, it feels just right.
A raccoon snickers, with mischievous glee,
While a butterfly lands, oh so free.

Mossy cushions for sitting down,
With squirrels wearing their nutty crowns.
The shadows giggle, just out of sight,
In this green haven, the mood feels light.

A rabbit hops by, all fluffy and bold,
With tales so funny, eagerly told.
Beneath rustling leaves, you'll find delight,
Where laughter dances, from morn to night.

So grab a friend, come join the fun,
In this leafy world, where joy has begun.
A haven of chuckles, secrets, and cheer,
In the heart of nature, let's make it clear!

Mysteries Beyond the Underbrush

Deep in the thickets, where shadows roam,
Lies a goofy gnome, far from home.
With a big red hat and mismatched shoes,
He tells the trees the funniest news.

Hidden treasures spark and tease,
While the grasshoppers giggle in the breeze.
A hedgehog chuckles, his quills a-fuzz,
While ants plot stories, just because.

A rustle reveals a curious hare,
With big bright eyes, do they really care?
He snickers softly, and hops in place,
Embracing the wild with a silly grace.

Each nibble and poke, a riddle unfolds,
Nature's magic, a sight to behold.
So let's explore, and uncover the fun,
In these mysteries, let laughter run!

The Lament of the Ancient Oak

Oh, the wise old oak, standing tall and true,
With branches like arms, waving to you.
He grumbles and groans, with stories of old,
Of squirrels who stole his acorns of gold.

He remembers the times when he was a sprout,
With dances by fairies, all twist and shout.
Now he just watches the world spin around,
As chipmunks invade his leafy crown.

Birds laugh at him, perched on a limb,
While below, a raccoon does a silly whim.
"Why so serious?" they tease and croon,
"Oh, lighten up, you'll be dancing soon!"

So he shakes his leaves, gives a chuckle deep,
In this forest realm, laughter's a leap.
Though the years have been many, the fun still remains,
In the heart of the woods, joy forever reigns.

The Lament of Lost Trails

Oh where have my feet taken me now,
A rabbit's tail or a cow's brown brow?
Paths twist and turn like a dervish's dance,
Yet I trip on twigs, not a hint of romance.

My map's lost its magic, my compass can't spin,
It points to a creek where I lost my left shoe.
I laugh at the squirrels, they seem to win,
While I'm snagged on a branch, feeling quite blue.

Shouts of confusion echo in trees,
As I bump into bushes and scramble with ease.
The shadowy green seems to laugh as I fall,
I wonder now if I'm just having a ball.

Yet in the midst of my goofy plight,
I find a wise owl who's laughing in flight.
With a wink and a hoot, he sums up my quest,
"Just enjoy the trip; the wrong way's the best!"

In Search of the Sylvan Muse

In the grove where the shadows play tricks,
I search for my genius; oh, where's my fix?
The trees hold secrets, but who's keeping score,
When a squirrel steals my snack? This is such a bore!

Oh Muse, are you hiding in branches so high?
I hear giggles and whispers—are they all a spy?
While I sit and ponder, the bees start to buzz,
They plot and they plan, just like me, what a fuss!

With laughter, my thoughts take a curious bend,
As mushrooms entice me, a colorful friend.
"Dance with the daisies!" they seem to insist,
But I trip on the grass, where'd I put my wrist?

Yet mirth fills the air with a joyful loud cheer,
As I tumble and giggle, confusion turns clear.
Each wobble I take is a step in the dance,
Maybe this forest is just a wise trance!

Aria of the Broken Branches

In a grove where the sunlight twirls in delight,
I found a sad branch that was broken, quite slight.
It creaked out a ballad of sorrowful plight,
As I chuckled out loud—what a comical sight!

With leaves in the breeze, it played a fine tune,
"Join me," it beckoned, "let's lift off to the moon!"
But I stepped in a puddle, and oh what a splash,
While the laughter of nature just made my heart thrash.

Amidst the tall pines, I twirled like a fool,
Drawing smiles from the dance of the old willow pool.
Each stumble a jest, each trip was a prize,
As the forest erupted in wild, gleeful sighs.

So here's to the branches that break, twist, and turn,
Their songs a reminder, a lesson to learn.
That joy often hides in the messes we make,
And laughter rings loud when the wilds start to quake!

Selkie's Song Beneath the Canopy

Beneath the green roof where the fairies convene,
I met a strange creature who danced in between.
With a flip of her tail, she splashed on the ground,
While I laughed so hard, I could hardly make sound.

"Come play in the puddles!" she sang with great cheer,
But my rubbery boots weren't built for this sphere.
I leapt like a salmon, fell flat on my face,
While the forest erupted in a fit of sheer grace.

"Can you be my muse?" she asked with a grin,
While I rolled in the mud, and she joined in my spin.
We laughed with the flowers and twirled 'round the trees,
While the sunbeams we caught danced like joyous bees.

So here's to the selkies and souls of the wood,
In laughter and splashes, we understood.
That playtime is magic beneath branches wide,
Where whimsy and joy walk hand in hand, side by side!

Footsteps on the Forest Floor

With each step, I slip and slide,
The ground a trampoline, oh what a ride!
Roots like snakes twist and twirl,
I step with grace, until I whirl.

A squirrel watches, munching his nut,
Laughing loud at my clumsy strut.
Branches overhead shake and sway,
As I question my path in a comical way.

A Journey Through Leafy Veils

Leaves whisper secrets, tickling my ear,
 I catch a bug, but it disappears.
Mushrooms pop up, all shaped like hats,
I wave to a toad; he jumps back, then chats.

Beneath the boughs, a rabbit hops near,
"Careful now!" I shout, "Don't get too near!"
He twitches his nose, and I just plead,
 "Borrow my shoes? You seem fast indeed!"

Mists in the Morning Glade

Fog hangs thick, like a cotton candy dream,
I trip over roots, my voice a loud scream.
A branch smacks my face—oh what a mess!
Nature's slapstick; I'm just wanting less stress!

But look, a deer with a prancing cheer,
Seems to chuckle, "What's the rush, my dear?"
I bow, quite grand, in a silly shrouded haze,
She snorts at my stance, then prances away.

Forgotten Groves and Hidden Streams

A grove of trees, standing quite tall,
I wave to the squirrels, they just stall.
Ducks in the brook quack out a tune,
I dance with the fish—oh, how they swoon!

Behind the bushes, I hear a loud splash,
It's a frog that's leaping, oh what a dash!
With giggles and hops, we share our day,
Nature's best jesters, come out and play!

Shadows and Sunbeams: A Forest Illusion

In the woods where the shadows play,
Sunbeams dance and have their say.
A squirrel in a tie takes a bow,
While birds gossip like they're in a row.

Trees whisper tales of yesterday,
While bushes giggle in a fray.
The hidden paths twist and turn,
And the leaves have secrets to discern.

Mushrooms wear hats all crooked and strange,
Outlaws of the forest, so they arrange.
Each footstep echoes a comical tune,
As critters waltz beneath the moon.

So chase those shadows, let the laughter ring,
In this woodland where the oddities swing.
With every twist, a jest awaits,
And a chipmunk chef transforms your plates.

The Allure of Moss-Covered Stones

Mossy rocks with a touch of grace,
Host a party in the shaded space.
Frogs in tuxedos croak with flair,
While snails debate the best kind of wear.

Each stone holds a secret, a tale to tell,
Of beetles that danced and drank too well.
With laughter bubbling like a brook,
Every nook and cranny hides a funny hook.

Wiggle your toes in the green delight,
As lizards perform in a spotlight.
The mossy stage, a comedic scene,
A clutch of leaves as their backdrop green.

So sit on a stone, let humor flow,
In this kingdom where surprises grow.
The forest floor giggles, can you hear?
Nature's jesters invite you near.

Tales of the Wandering Bark

Once a piece of bark set out on a quest,
To find a tree that dressed the best.
It tried on leaves and a sturdy branch,
In a barky ballet, it took a chance.

With every step, the critters sighed,
As the ferns swayed, and the pine trees cried.
The bark became famous, what a delight!
A fashion icon under the moonlight.

Rabbits critiqued its outfit so wild,
While beetles applauded, oh, how they smiled!
But the bark in the end just wanted to stay,
Rooted in laughter, no runway display.

So gather 'round for this bark's funny show,
In the forest of quirk where the oddballs grow.
With every giggle, a new tale sparks,
In the land where humor meets the barks.

A Breeze of Secrets Between the Trees

A breeze whistles tunes through the leafy band,
Delivering gossip from tree to hand.
The flowers blush as secrets unfold,
While the dandelions burst, oh, so bold.

A Parrot with shades claims he's the boss,
While rabbits argue who's the true floss.
Each gust carries tales both silly and slick,
As the whispers twirl, nature's own trick.

Owl winks knowingly from a perch above,
As the forest buzzes, a symphonic love.
With each gust of wind, laughter ignites,
Bringing bright chuckles through day and night.

So listen close, dear friend of the wood,
For the secrets abound where the funny stood.
With every breeze, another giggle stirs,
In the land where humor and wildlife blurs.

Parables of the Forest Floor

In the woods, leaves whisper loud,
Squirrels debate, oh so proud.
A fox tells tales, quite absurd,
Of a rabbit who forgot its word.

Mushrooms dance in the dappled light,
While crickets throw a banjo night.
Every shadow has a story true,
Even the ants are in on the view.

A raccoon wears a crown of twigs,
Proclaims he's king of dancing jigs.
But when he slips, oh what a sight,
The forest erupts in sheer delight!

With every rustle, laughter rings,
Nature's jesters do funny things.
So join the fun, don't be a bore,
Come frolic on the forest floor.

Twilight in the Thicket

As daylight fades, the shadows creep,
A hedgehog yawns, it's time for sleep.
But wait! A party starts to grow,
With fireflies putting on a show.

Bats swing low, like acrobats,
While owls hoot in fancy hats.
The crickets form a lively band,
Playing tunes upon the sand.

A deer prances with awkward grace,
Chasing shadows, lost in the chase.
A raccoon sneaks in for a bite,
Stealing snacks, oh what a night!

The thicket hums with playful cheer,
As twilight casts its magic here.
In this wild dance, all is well,
With giggles woven through the spell.

The Heartbeat of the Wild

In the wild, where laughter flows,
The heartbeat skips, and mischief grows.
A beaver builds, but can't find the wood,
As a laughing chipmunk thinks he could.

A snake on a branch, he tries to pose,
But forgets he's got a ticklish nose.
He sneezes loud, a startled deer,
Jumps so high, it's quite a cheer!

A hedgehog rolls into a ball,
And ends up with leaves—a prickly shawl.
The forest chuckles, a silly sight,
Where critters share their joyful plight.

So listen close to nature's beat,
In every laugh, the wild's a treat.
With stories spun beneath the stars,
The rhythm of life is full of jars.

Through the Eyes of the Untamed

Oh, the sights from up a tree,
Where squirrels nod, and whispers flee.
A bunny hops, but then loses track,
While a crow caws, "You can't go back!"

The stream giggles as it flows,
Telling tales that no one knows.
A turtle grins, slow but wise,
Dreaming big 'neath the sunny skies.

A wild thing stumbles, then finds its flair,
Dancing 'round without a care.
The muddled paths lead to silly turns,
Where every wild creature learns.

In every glance, wild stories bloom,
Life's antics brighten up the gloom.
So embrace the fun in each untamed sigh,
For nature's magic is never shy.

In Pursuit of Feathered Dreams

A parrot passed my ear with flair,
It thought my hat was quite a chair.
I chased it through the thickened trees,
Dodging squirrels with acorn keys.

The crow made faces, cawed in jest,
As I tripped over a worm's fest.
A peacock strutted, all in blues,
While I wore mud like pretty shoes.

The owls just hooted, wise and bold,
"Why chase the birds? Just sip your cold!"
But I was smitten by the flight,
In pursuit of dreams both day and night.

At last I find, my heart now glows,
A feather stuck upon my nose.
I laugh and dance in dirt and glee,
Alive in nature, wild and free.

Secrets Etched in Bark and Stone

In ancient woods where trees stand tall,
I found a message carved on a wall.
But it was just a heart with eyes,
Signed 'I love pizza' – what a surprise!

Rocks whispered tales of times gone by,
Not of kings, but of a pie.
The mushrooms laughed, as I stood still,
Sipping dew from a daffodil.

One squirrel claimed to guard a nest,
But held his breath, he couldn't rest.
"Don't tell the fox about my stash!"
Then dashed away in a swift flash.

So secrets hidden in nature's fold,
Are often silly, never old.
For every grove and every stone,
Hides laughter that's equally well-known.

Serpentine Paths of the Unknown

The path twisted like a playful snake,
I stumbled upon a giant cake.
Frogs in hats threw quite a bash,
As hedgehogs served up cookies in a flash.

A rabbit asked if I had spare cheese,
While bees debated on how to tease.
I laughed aloud, it felt so weird,
My sandwich vanished, was I that feared?

The trail grew wild, and so did I,
Trying to fly, I just did a sigh.
Lizards chuckled, scaling trees high,
While I was busy munching on pie.

But in the chaos, joy came alive,
A taste of whimsy, I began to thrive.
With serpentine paths, a humorous quest,
Took me to treasures, and I loved it best.

Embraced by Shadows and Sunlight

Sunlight danced on leaves up high,
While shadows played a hide-and-sigh.
An ant in sunglasses walked on by,
Claiming he was king of the fry!

Bumblebees buzzed their rhythmical tunes,
While chipmunks jived under paper moons.
I found a shadow that looked quite bright,
A mismatched sock, a comical sight.

As I ventured further, what did I see?
A turtle yoga class, all 'Om' and glee.
The tiniest critters joined the fun,
As sunlight melted into the run.

Embraced by laughter, both dark and light,
The woods sang softly, oh what a sight!
In this jolly escape, I felt the sway,
With shadows and sunlight, I danced away.

Whispers Through the Thicket

Where squirrels debate on what's nuts today,
A deer rolls its eyes at the showy display.
That bird's off-key, yet it draws quite a crowd,
Even the trees seem to giggle out loud.

The path is a twist, like a noodle uncooked,
While rabbits are plotting—do they have a book?
A raccoon in shades gives a smirk and a wink,
As I pause for a moment to ponder and think.

Through bushes that rustle with secrets untold,
A fox pulls a prank on the overconfident bold.
With chatter so loud from the critters around,
Nature's the jest in this wild, merry ground.

If laughter could echo through leaves up above,
The joy of the wildwood is what we all love.
So tiptoe with glee where the funny things thrive,
In thickets and shadows, we come alive!

Echoes of the Untamed Path

A turtle named Larry claimed he's quite fast,
Declaring a race, but he finished last.
While birds tease the beetles for their slow little crawl,
It's a slowpoke parade; they're having a ball.

The river sings songs of the silliness near,
Where frogs throw a party, and all show up here.
With hiccups from toads and a splash from the brook,
Each ripple and giggle's a wide-open book.

In shadows of ferns, a debate springs to life,
Who's the best dancer, a rabbit or wife?
The groundhogs just chuckle, they've seen it before,
As they munch on some clover and wait for encore.

So follow the echoes, let laughter take flight,
In forests of humor, where whimsy ignites.
Each step is a treasure, a joy to be found,
In this quirky old realm where the funny abounds!

Beneath the Canopy's Embrace

Beneath leaves' green shelter, the sun starts to wink,
Where raccoons are scheming, and squirrels just drink.
A parrot named Polly tells jokes with great flair,
And even the snails start a dance unaware.

The owls wear their glasses, so wise and so grand,
Though they end up in mishaps; oh isn't it grand?
They hoot and they holler when caught out with flair,
In the wild's little theater, there's laughter to share.

With shadows and whispers, the mischief runs deep,
As crickets play music, while rabbits just leap.
Each flower's a giggle, each twig's one more pun,
In this playful green world where laughter's the fun.

So bask in the foolishness soft as a breeze,
In a canopy rich with the quirkiest tease.
Each step brings a chuckle, a story anew,
In this wild place of giggles, there's always a view!

Secrets of the Forest Floor

Upon the soft carpet where mushrooms have grown,
A beetle's a king on a throne made of stone.
The ants are the jesters, they dance 'round the mound,
In a whispering realm, where sweet laughter's found.

The grass is a giggle, each blade has a tale,
Of hopping and laughing through sun and through hail.
A wise old tortoise with jokes in his shell,
Recites all the secrets he knows very well.

The bog's got its quirks, where the frogs make a scene,
With splashes and croaks that are fit for a queen.
Each puddle reflects all the joy that we seek,
With dance parties happening every other week.

So join in the revels, take joy in the jest,
In this land of giggles, we're truly blessed.
With mischief and magic under skies so grand,
Secrets of laughter writ large through the land!

www.ingramcontent.com/pod-product-compliance
Lightning Source LLC
Chambersburg PA
CBHW072147200426
43209CB00051B/825